LIGHT WAYS

Tools of Space Creation and Energy
to Manifest Peace, Power and Abundance

Diana McLellan

First published 2021

Text copyright © Diana McLellan 2021
The moral right of the author has been asserted

All rights reserved. No part of this publication may be reproduced, stored in a retrieval system, or transmitted in any form or by any means, electronic, mechanical, photocopying, recording or otherwise, without the prior written permission of the publisher and copyright holder.

A self published title
Designed and produced by Adala Publishing
www.adala.com.au

 A catalogue record for this book is available from the National Library of Australia

ISBN 978-0-6453485-0-7 (Print)
ISBN 978-0-6453485-1-4 (eBook)

DEDICATION

This book is my gift of love and possibility to
my children Elise, Alexander and Wendy
and to all whom I love
and to all those of you who may
choose to read it.

ACKNOWLEDGEMENTS

Thanks be for all the loving support I have and do receive from Jim, Elise, Alexander and Wendy, Khemar and Mark. Thanks be also for the forever encouragement of Lynette, David and Elizabeth and the many blessings of loving friends.

I am so fortunate for having been introduced to Sonya Murphy, Adala Publishing and for her attention to detail, her always committed support, expertise, professionalism and guidance towards the best production of this book and all the many facets that surround this project. Thankyou Sonya.

Thanks be to all those who have and will play their part in making real for me a kaleidoscope of human experience and for the many joys and life lessons along the way.

Thanks be also to the Higher Energies of Love and Light that always travel with, protect, inspire, encourage and guide me even when I may not be aware of it.

QUOTES

"If you wish to understand the Universe, think of energy, frequency and vibration" – Nikola Tesla.

"Our entire biological system, the brain and the earth itself, work on the same frequencies" – Nikola Tesla.

"Our mind is only a receiver. We just need to tune it with the Universe" – Nikola Tesla.

"Everything is energy and that's all there is to it" – Albert Einstein.

"Imagination is more important than knowledge. Imagination is the language of the soul. Pay attention to your imagination and you will discover all you need to be fulfilled". – Albert Einstein.

"Strive not to be a success, but to be of value" – Albert Einstein.

"What you seek is seeking you" – Rumi

"Everything in the Universe is within you. Ask all from yourself"
– Rumi

"You are the Universe expressing itself as a human for a little while"
– Eckhart Tolle.

CONTENTS

INTRODUCTION	1
Energy	1
The Energetic Nature of a Human Being	3
Intention	5
You	6
The Angelic Realms	7
What is Space Creation Useful For? How Can it Improve Your Daily Life?	7
ENERGETIC SPACES AND BOUNDARIES	10
The Anatomy of the Personal, Work and World Space	10
A Designated Space for Elements	10
A Designated Space for Creation Symbols	11
Claim and Create your Spaces and Boundaries	13
How to Objectify Energy Forms in Order to Better Work With Them	14
Discernment	14
PERSONAL SPACE	16
Method For Creating your Personal Space	16
1. Claim your Personal Space	16
2. Conscious Connection to The Divine	16
3. Clear your Personal Space	18

4. Seal your Personal Space	19
5. The Portal of your Personal Space	19
6. Add Creation Symbols	20
7. Run the Light	20
Using the Breath	22
Using a Mantra	22
8. Thanks be for the Creation of your Personal Space	23

WORK SPACE   24

Definition and Uses of a Work Space	24
Rehearsal	24
Creation	24
Peace	24
Acknowledgement vs Connection	25
Security and Choice	25
Method	25
Healing For Self and Others, Near and Distant	27
Respect	27
Method For Creating Your Work Space	28
1. Claim	28
2. Clear and Seal. Add The Portal	28
3. Connection	29
4. Introduce Creation Symbols and Other Supported Players	30
5. Run The Light	30
6. Thanks Be	31
7. Completion	31
Method for Completion	31
Example 1 – Creating this Book in My Study Work Space	32
Example 2 – Meetings and Appointments	35

WORLD SPACE	**36**
Definition and Uses of a World Space	36
Opening Up	36
Ease and Relaxation	37
Gift to Others	37
Size	37
Nature	37
Mini-World Spaces	37
Planet Earth	38
Method For Creating a World Space	38
1. Claim	38
2. Clear and Seal. Add The Portal	38
3. Connect	38
4. Run The Light	38
5. Thanks Be	38
6. Completion	39
Example 1 – Driving	39
Example 2 – Orchestral Performance	39
SPACES AS A TOOL	**41**
1. Manifestation Tool	41
2. Daily Meditation Practice	42
3. For Right Relationship	42
Uses of Spaces and How to Objectify Energy, as a Relationship Tool	46
Gift of Love and Light	46
Self-knowledge and Understanding	46
Discernment	46
Personal Power	46
Compassion and Forgiveness	46

Method For Using Space Creation and Energy as a Relationship Tool	47
1. Space Creation	47
2. Objectify Energy as a Form or Shape	47
3. Enclose, Post and Return Sender	47
4. Next Best Action?	48
5. Reclarify and Reset any Personal or Work Space Boundaries, if necessary	48
6. Thanks Be	50
Example 1 – Work Meeting Presentation	50
Example 2 – Driving cont.	52
4. For Health Creation	53
Best Medical Practice	53
Self-Responsibility	53
Growth	54
Example – Neck-jam	54
Method for Unravelling, Using a <u>Healing Meditation</u>	55
Breathing in Nature From Within My Work and World Spaces	56
Method For Unravelling, Using a <u>Drawing Technique</u>	58
1. What is So Now?	58
2. What Do You Choose to Create?	59
3. What Do I Need to Do Now?	59
1. Post it.	59
2. Messages or A New Mantra?	59
4. Next Best Action?	59
1. Breathe	59
2. Add Creation Symbol	60
3. Further Messages or Mantras	60
5. Breathe and Run The Light	60
6. Thanks Be	60

5. For Wealth Creation	62
Method for Creating Wealth	63
Space Creation – Personal Space	63
Space Creation – Work Space	63
Method:	
1. Make Your Work Space	63
2. Add Elements	63
3. Creation Symbols	63
4. Connect	63
5. Run The Light	63
Working with your Creation Symbols	64
Method:	64
1. See, Feel, Speak	64
2. Next Best Action?	64
3. Releasing Lower Energy Thoughtforms from Creation Symbols	65
Method:	65
1. Objectify	65
2. Unravel	66
3. Post	66
4. Messages, Next Best Actions or Mantras	66
5. Re-Speak	66
6. Run the Light	66
7. Thanks be	66
Example – Unravelling for the Successful Sale of our Home Using a Drawing Technique	66
1. What is so Now?	66
2. What Do I Now Choose to Create?	68
3. What do I need to do Now? Post it.	68

4. Next Best Action? 69
   Messages 69
   Mantras 69
5. Run The Light 70
6. Thanks be 70
A note on choosing end results 70

DIVINE TIMING AND CONCLUSION 72

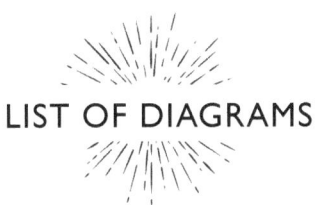

LIST OF DIAGRAMS

Note: I have purposefully left all diagrams in their original hand-drawn form so that you can readily see that the methods I share with you require only whatever written and drawn expression is meaningful and personal to you. I have typed up some of the written information within some of the diagrams for the purpose of legibility only.

No artistic skill or degree of perfection is required to successfully engage with any of the processes offered in this book.

p. 5	**Diagram 1**	The Divine Energy Creation-Sources of a Human Being.
p. 12	**Diagram 2a**	Anatomy of a Personal, Work and World Space.
	Diagram 2b	How all Relevant Elements and Players within a Work Space are Interconnected Through Source.
p. 13	**Diagram 2c**	How The Centre of a Work Space Is a Focus Area and Screen for Specific Enquiry or Attention.
p. 15	**Diagram 3**	Examples: Different Ways Lower Energy Thoughtforms and Reactions Can Be Given a Shape or Physical Form.
p. 17	**Diagram 4**	The Vertical Flow of Divine Energy Through Consciously Created Spaces.
p. 21	**Diagram 5**	Running The Light While Lying Down and While Upright.
p. 26	**Diagram 6**	Acknowledgement vs Connection With Others.
p. 29	**Diagram 7**	The Energetic Maypole Within a Work Space Where Elements and Creation Symbols for your Chosen End Results are all Connected Through Source.

p. 31	**Diagram 8**	The Energetic Maypole Within a Personal Space Where Elements and Creation Symbols for your Chosen End Results are all Connected Through Source.
p. 33	**Diagram 9**	Example: Creation Symbols for Worldwide 1 Successful Publication and Contribution to Others of this Book. 2 Right Audience, Readership.
p. 34	**Diagram 10**	Example: Work Space for the Successful Writing, Publication and Contribution of this Book.
p. 40	**Diagram 11**	Example: Setting Up Elements and Intentions for an Uplifting Orchestral Performance Using Designated Spaces.
p. 45	**Diagram 12**	Personal Spaces in Right Relationship and When Personal Spaces are Collapsed, Either Consciously or Unconsciously.
p. 49	**Diagram 13**	Enclose, Post, Return Sender of Lower Energy Thoughtforms from: 1 Another Person. 2 A Passing Lower Energy Thoughtform Cloud.
p. 61	**Diagram 14**	Example – Neck-Jam. The Unravelling Process Using a Drawing Technique.
p. 67	**Diagram 15**	Example – Sale of Our House. The Unravelling Process Using A Drawing Technique.
p. 71	**Diagram 16**	The Effect of Being on Different Energetic Highways for Manifesting Outcomes and End Results.

INTRODUCTION

What follows is a sharing of my truth and beliefs only. I share with you because I have come to A Way that works for me and now offer it to you in case it could make a difference for you too.

Energy

This book is about how to consciously engage with the unseen player or force that is at work in our world that is called energy. I see energy as the creator that forms all within our physical, mental, emotional and spiritual worlds.

I believe that there are unseen energies and energy forms, including those that are sourced from our minds and imagination. I believe that there is also a master Universal energy which is, in essence Divine of nature and is one of pure Love and Light. I will use the terms (The) Source, Higher Energy, (The) Light, Divine Spirit, Universal Energy or God interchangeably to refer to this Divine energy of Love and Light. Anything less than Love and Light I say we as human beings have created, believe in and perpetuate. I call these man-made energies Lower Energy Thoughtforms. I term the energies that arise from the Divine as Higher Energy Thoughtforms.

For me, one of our tasks as human beings is to consciously acknowledge and perceive these Lower Energy Thoughtforms and to choose for the Truth of Love and Light. This requires us to have knowledge about how to consciously and successfully engage with energy, energy forms and The Light.

This book deals with how to consciously manage energy in all its forms, for the Highest Good of yourself and others, through the purposeful creation of Spaces. Specifically, your Personal Space, your Work Space(s) and your World Space.

This book offers you a chance to try on witnessing the nature of energy forms in your life and how to use energy to consciously create and manifest whatever may be your desired and chosen end results; indeed, to be receptive to all your Highest Good. In the process of exploring the methods I will share with you, you will see and feel for yourself what works best for you. If this approach does not call to, or resonate with you, know that you shall surely be guided to what shall.

I do not claim this method and the beliefs around it to be the Truth, but only a possibility that I pursue, hold as my truth, and that works well for me at this time. You do not need to agree with, or to adopt my beliefs in order to make use of the methods and techniques I shall present to you.

Please note that this way of working with energy is not intended to be used as an alternative to responsible medical care. Although it could well be used in conjunction with mainstream healthcare practitioners.

....

Example

Before I go to the dentist I will, in my imagination preset the surgery as a Work Space (see p. 24). That is, I define the boundaries of the space, clear it and then connect myself and the dentist and their assistant to the Divine Source that we are to share. I choose that all that occurs in that dental session will be given with the greatest care, gentleness and ease and with the best practice. I select a mantra for the dental session such as '…that was easy!'. I form a clear feeling-image of being relaxed while receiving treatment, and of feeling happy and relieved that all was well done as I am leaving the dentist's surgery.

These are the images and mantra I hold to, and give my attention and energy to, before and during the upcoming dental session. There is always choice; do you choose to energize thoughts of fear and pain, or do you choose to energize thoughts of ease, confidence and trust?

....

As in all things it is always your responsibility to take best care of your well-being, to respect the well-being of others and to always seek professional advice and support when appropriate.

The Energetic Nature of a Human Being

My premise as to the nature of the human being is that we are spiritual beings experiencing the human form and condition. We also have the added, particularly human faculties, of being able to be aware and *conscious* of our inner life, as well as to what is going on outside of us. Further we have the critical faculty of *choice*.

My equation for the conscious human being could be expressed thus:

A Conscious Human Being = Body, Mind, Emotions
+ Awareness
+ Choice
+ Divine Spirit.

We are each a unique living physical form that is a meeting of the Divine Spirit and all that the human condition holds – the physical body, the human emotional and mental body and a psyche of awareness and choice.

Our spiritual self gives us access to witnessing and working with the unseen forces of energy and of the Love and Light that I believe permeate all this world and the Universe. Our physical self enables us to consciously experience and enjoy all that comes with having a body and this human life.

This duality occurs when we are conceived and born as a point of Light, a star, onto this Earth upon a ray of Divine Light that emanates from the great mystery of The Source. This gives us our immediate and forever spiritual beingness and connection.

Many believe that our individual Divine star-point of creation dwells in our hearts. Similarly, one can say that there is a creation star-point at the centre or heart of our planet, which gives it its life and form.

Our physical human form is made of and from this Earth. It is a gift to us from the star of Light, The Source that resides in and creates our Earth and all upon it.

*(See **Diagram 1**. The Divine Energetic Creation Source of a Human Being)*
Note: I have purposefully left all diagrams in their original hand-drawn form so that you can readily see that the methods I share with you require only whatever written and drawn expression is meaningful and personal to you. I have typed up some of the written information within some of the diagrams for the purpose of legibility only.

No artistic skill or degree of perfection is required to successfully engage with any of the processes offered in this book.

I believe that we are as a single beam of Light that is born from the Creator, that is connected to us at the point of our hearts, and then to the Earth from which we are physically formed. I see human beings as many beams of Light radiating upon our planet, akin to the drop of water that dwells in an ocean, a mere particle of something far greater.

Our task seems to be to consciously know and work with both aspects of our beingness. This requires us to bring conscious awareness to both sides of our nature. On the one hand, we have access to the whispers and guidance of our Higher spiritual selves and all the joy and love that emanates from it. On the other hand, we can allow and experience in our body, mind and emotions, all the outcomes of the choices that the fullness of our human condition offers us.

In so doing we bring to the table such qualities as acceptance, compassion and choice for our humanity and to surrender, trust, peace and confidence in the Divine Plan. When we consciously choose for the highest that we can be, we can follow the truth of our joy and become more aware of the nature of the unique gifts that we came to this Earth to share for the benefit of all.

Heaven Source

Earth Source

Diagram 1 The Divine Energy Creation-Sources of a Human Being.

Intention

The intention of this book is to give you a simple, clear and easy introduction into how to consciously use your imagination to enhance your actual and your sense of power in your world. This can be done through objectively witnessing energy forms at play in your life and then managing these energy forms using conscious Space Creation and choice.

I have purposefully slowed down the techniques I employ into their sequential parts so that they can be more fully understood and followed. What may seem complex, is in fact accomplished in milli-seconds with one's imagination and intention.

The intention of this book is to give you the power to be in your peace no matter where you may be, or how you may feel, and to successfully create and manifest whatever it is you choose. You have the power to manage your inner or outer conflicts more effectively. You have the power to witness the nature of shifting energy and energy forms consciously and compassionately within your and others' Spaces. Whenever you exercise your power of choice for more love and light in your personal world, you also make shine more brightly the love and light for all upon this world called Earth.

You

It all begins with you. It begins with taking responsibility for, and having compassion for, the human condition you inhabit and with which you navigate this world.

It will require you to use your imagination to work consciously and purposefully with this energy force as the co-creator that you are. Know that throughout this process you are being held and guided by Divine energies for the Highest Good of yourself and others. You cannot get it wrong, for we are always learning and refining what works best for us. Given the opportunity, I believe that we all strive towards bringing more creativity, love, light, joy and peace to ourselves, to those around us and to our world. When we are conscious of our Divine nature, when we can know ourselves to be powerful co-creators, why would we choose anything other? It seems to be that it is only when we fall into reaction, or into the unconscious abyss of our human animal selves, that our base instincts dominate our choices.

The Angelic Realms

Our imagination is one of our most powerful tools, but I also believe that the angelic realms can be and are an amazing, readily available source of support in our lives. For example, I will use my imagination to choose, see and feel the perimeter of the Space I wish to create and *then* I will ask Archangel Michael to secure this perimeter with his protective Light and to blast this created Space with his clearing Light energy. You could use any Higher Energy of your choice to support you.

You do not need to believe in the angelic realms, or to request their assistance for the methods of Space Creation and energy work to be effective. You only need to use your imagination, your intention, and conscious choices to successfully work with any of the tools I describe in this book. My relationship with the angelic and Higher realms is a personal, spiritual one and is not based on any religious teachings.

What is Space Creation Useful For? How Can it Improve Your Daily Life?

Here are some of the ways you can successfully use Space Creation to manage the quality of the energy within consciously defined Spaces, and to move towards the creation and manifestation of whatever may be your chosen end results.

All the possible ways you can use energy and Space Creation require you to first make conscious choices and then to accept that there are unknowable forces at play, to which you have always been connected and that are always working on your behalf.

Space Creation and working with energy heightens connection with your own intuition and wisdom. It also increases your receptivity and clarity to your current energetic condition, as well as to any energetic affect others may be having upon you.

It is useful to be able to distinguish what energetic thought or feeling belongs to, and is currently active in you, from that which has been triggered, mirrored from or taken on from another. To so distinguish becomes a platform for understanding and compassion for what is the current condition and experience of another. It is not your responsibility to react to or take on others' energy forms or to fix them. This is the other's responsibility. As it is your responsibility to manage your own energetic condition.

Even so, all reactions or resonations to parts of your humanity you deem bad and wrong, are opportunities to own your humanity with acceptance and peace, and to let these Lower Energy Thoughtforms pass you by, to go back into the ethers from where they came. When you bring awareness to your reactivity, or to your susceptibility to taking on energies from others, you can then consciously shift them to the Light. This will bring you much relief, peace and power.

Specifically, here are some of the possible benefits that working with Spaces and energy can bring you in all areas your life – relationships, health, wealth and career.

1. **Relationships** – personal, in business and with The Divine. To create a safe, empowering space for yourself to inhabit; setting up an environment for fun and **'right relationship'** (p. 43); speaking your truth freely and clearly and in peace whether in person or not; conflict resolution; to maintain distance from unwanted situations or people when necessary; a way to quickly and safely unravel (p. 55, 58), understand and heal your reactions with clarity; growth of clarity in your Higher Self intuition and your connection and trust in co-creating with The Divine Source.
2. **Health** – personal and for others, near or distant; to achieve health goals, or when working with health professionals; releasing all that does not serve you; allowing support from those others who resonate with you, to be successful and to flow with ease; to communicate

with your body as to its needs and why it may be presenting you with health issues; to be able to scan your physical body energetically.

3. **Wealth and Career** – To choose end results or outcomes for yourself; knowing your Next Best Actions; setting up an environment for best productivity; teamwork while staying connected to your and others' Highest guidance; brain-storming solutions; staying on track with working towards consciously chosen group outcomes and taking responsibility for, and releasing of, any reactionary responses; release of disempowering reactions or sabotage thoughts or procrastination habits.

ENERGETIC SPACES AND BOUNDARIES

The Anatomy of The Personal, Work and World Space

Your Personal Space, Work Space and World Space all share the same construction or features; a Divine Boundary, a Divine Portal and a variety of Designated Spaces for the Elements and Creation Symbols that you have chosen to work with in a Space. All within a Space are connected to Source and thereby to each other. The area at the centre of every Work and World Space is left purposefully open to function as a Focus Circle where specific Elements or Creation Symbols can be explored individually.
*(See **Diagrams 2a, b & c** pp. 12–13)*

A Designated Space for Elements

A Designated Space can contain either Elements or Creation Symbols. Elements would include the Personal Spaces of anyone (who I refer to as Players) you would like to specifically work with, or that you feel would best support you at this time. Examples of this would be living or deceased sources of wisdom and Higher Energies. Another element that may be of interest to you would be to have a specific Healing Circle that you could use and work within for yourself and for others. Elements sit closest to the outer perimeter of the boundary of your Work and World Spaces, as if overseeing all within them.

I find Elements are best situated **only** in Work and World Spaces. Your Personal Space is *your personal space* and I choose that none other reside within it other than my chosen Creation Symbols and the cord and the vertical conduit of Light that is my Divine connection.

A Designated Space for Creation Symbols

Apart from housing various Elements, a Designated Space can also be used to contain one's Creation Symbols (p. 30), i.e. those symbols that represent what you now choose to manifest in your life, your desired end results or outcomes. I will position any Creation Symbols the next level in from the Element Spaces. Notice that Creation Symbols are included and placed into all your Spaces; your Personal, Work and World Spaces.

To recapitulate, the common anatomy of all Spaces are:
- *The Divine Boundary.* The Divine boundary defines the perimeter of the Space.
- *The Divine Portal.* A **one-way** Portal that is an opening in the boundary of every Space through which anything unwanted, or that needs to be sent to the Light, can pass through.
- *The Designated Spaces* are variously used to contain Creation Symbols; **or** Elements for whatever or whomever as in those Players you wish to join and best support you on this project or earth journey; **or** for specific task spaces, such as in the Healing Circle Designated Space. Each Designated Space is connected to Source through a cord of Light which then enables interconnection to all within the Space.
- *The Focus Circle* is situated at the centre of each Work and World Space for bringing particular attention to a subject or person.

*(See **Diagram 2a**. Anatomy of a Personal, Work and World Space.*
***Diagram 2b**. How All Relevant Elements and Players within a Work Space are Interconnected Through Source. **Diagram 2c**. How The Centre of a Work Space Is a Focus Area and Screen for Specific Enquiry or Attention.)*

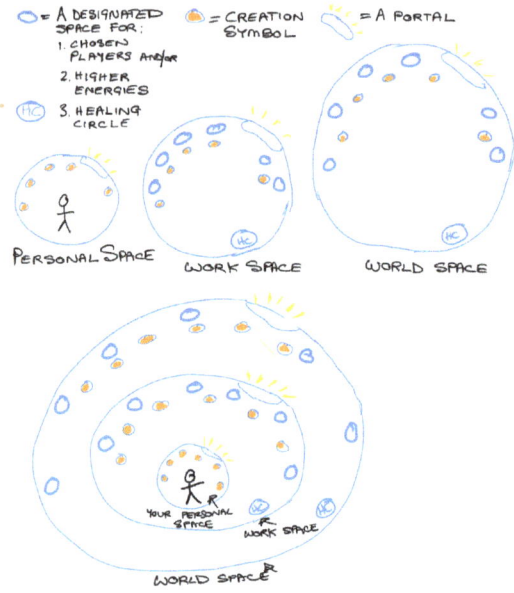

Diagram 2a Anatomy of a Personal, Work and World Space.

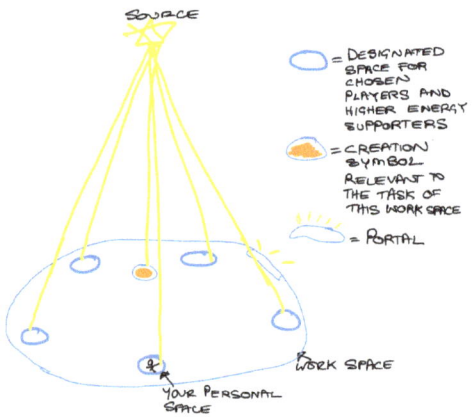

Diagram 2b How All Relevant Elements and Players within a Work Space are Interconnected Through Source.

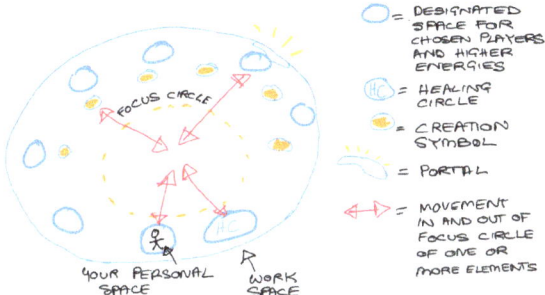

Diagram 2c How The Centre of a Work Space is A Focus Area and Screen for Specific Enquiry or Attention.

Claim and Create your Spaces and Boundaries

The first thing you will need to do in this process is to consciously claim and create your Spaces. There are three spaces I create and work with when necessary – your Personal Space, your Work Space and a World Space.

Even though we are all One at the spiritual level, we are also living a human life. This gives our human experience a sense of being separate to other humans and to the other forms that inhabit this Earth space. The creation and use of Spaces enable our human selves to be able to better consciously accept and work with both our humanness, as well as with the Divine part of our nature.

Decide for yourself how much space you would like or need to claim and own in order to live and work peacefully at this point in time. The size of these spaces may well change throughout the day according to your experienced needs and choices. These Spaces are solely for you to personally inhabit and to use (for the Highest Good of all concerned of course).

You are the **only** authority on how your Spaces are to be used. This applies equally to all your chosen Spaces – your Personal Space, your Work Space and to your World Space.

The process of claiming and owning is a mental one, using your imagination. It is a process for consciously making boundaries to what you will and will not allow passage into your chosen Spaces.

How to Objectify Energy Forms in order to Work With them

Once you have set your Spaces, then you can more readily observe the different unseen energies that may be at play in those Spaces.

I give energies a form, what I call an energyform or a thoughtform, by intuitively giving them a shape. In this way energies such as emotions are taken out of the body and the mind and externalized on paper or seen in one's imagination. It is far easier, I have found, to explore and work with emotional energyforms in this way; to be able to witness and unravel (p. 55, 58) them from a distance, so to speak.

There is no right way to give energy and thoughtforms a shape, it is purely an expression of how you are feeling in that moment. At another time you may choose to express these feelings differently. Once it is objectified you can work with it.

Discernment

It is very useful to know and be able to better distinguish what energyforms and thoughtforms

1. belong to us; from
2. those that we may be resonating to and that are in fact active within another; from
3. those that may have been directed at us, whether consciously or not, from another; from

4. those that may merely be passing us by in the ethers.

*(See **Diagram 3**. Different Ways Lower Energy Thoughtforms and Reactions can be given a Shape or Physical Form)*

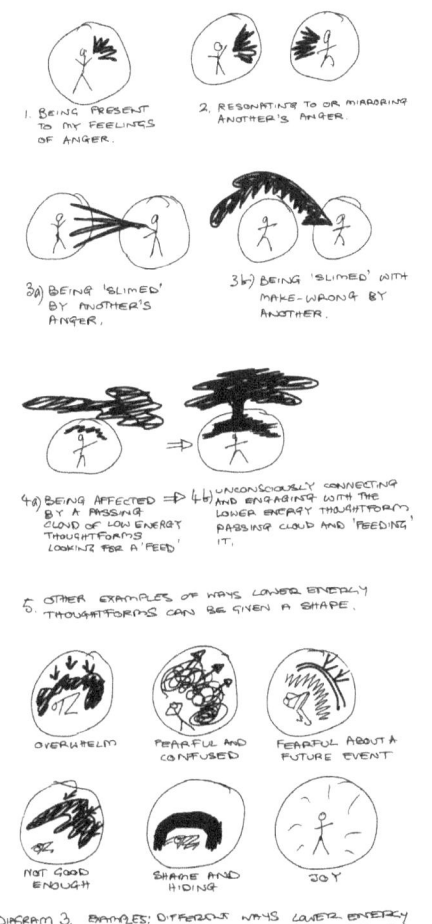

Diagram 3 <u>Examples:</u> Different Ways Lower Energy Thoughtforms and Reactions Can Be Given a Shape or Physical Form.

PERSONAL SPACE

Method for Creating your Personal Space

1. Claim your Personal Space

Look around you. How much space do you need at this moment in time to feel confident and at peace? Choose and make a mental circumference on the floor and let this perimeter become the basis for the size of your personal bubble or Space. **Note:** The bubble or Space you have just created extends not only above you but also in equal measure below you into the ground.

Choose and know that none other except Love and Light is given permission to energetically cross the boundary of this bubble of Light, your Personal Space. This is your personal boundary.

Anything or anyone can be given a Designated Space, a Personal Space. Sometimes you will find it useful to contain an idea, object, problem or an end result within its own Designated Personal Space. Explanations later. See Using Your Work Space (p. 23).

2. Conscious Connection to The Divine

When you create this Divine Personal Space you are also immediately setting up an individual continuous vertical conduit, like a Light-cylinder pathway that connects your human form to your Source in the heavens and to the core of this earth from where your physical form arises.

You are born as a spark of Divine Light originating from both the Heaven and the Earth Source. This can be seen and represented as a golden cord that connects your human form at the point of your heart to both the heavenly Source and to the Divine Source within this Earth.

So here you find yourself in a human form within the bubble of your unique sacred Personal Space that itself sits within a vertical *stream* of Divine Light, further connected to Source through a continuous golden *cord* of Light.

*(See **Diagram 4**. The Vertical Flow of Divine Energy Through Consciously Created Spaces)*

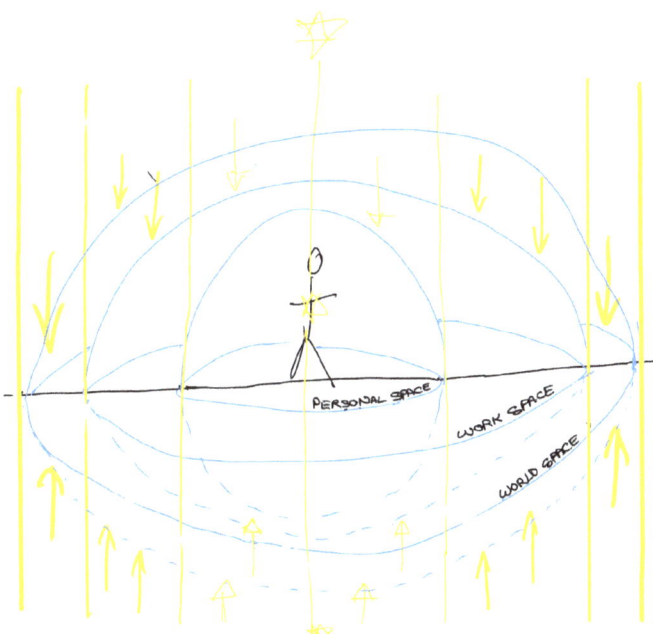

Diagram 4 The Vertical Flow of Divine Energy Through Consciously Created Spaces.

Note: if it feels easier, once you have chosen your personal circumference boundary upon the floor, you can let this immediately become the walls to your vertical conduit to the Source above and below. Then after you have done that, you can give yourself a top and a bottom to contain your unique human being within – to finish the creation of your personal egg or bubble. I find I switch the order of this creation process of my Personal Space from time to time, for no discernible reason other than it feels right. Sometimes I just need to first feel and be present to the flood of Divine Love and Light that flows through the conduit of my Personal Space. I would in this case, complete my bubble thereafter.

3. Clear your Personal Space

You use your imagination and intention to set the perimeter of your Personal Space and then to see or feel it being cleared with a blast of Light energy.

I prefer and find it quick and easy to *call in* and use the bright blue Light of Archangel Michael to form this bubble perimeter. This happens automatically, immediately upon making a request of Archangel Michael.

I then ask Archangel Michael to blast the contents of my Personal Space with white Light to clear it of all that is not of Love and Light. This occurs in an instant and appears to me like a flash of Divine protective white Light.

Note: You do not need to call in Archangel Michael. You could use whatever Higher Energy works for you or you may feel more comfortable and prefer to use your imagination and intention to claim and clear your Personal Space (or any other Space). There is no right way, whatever works best for you.

4. Seal your Personal Space

I also ask Archangel Michael to ensure all boundaries created are permeable only to Love and Light. I see the boundary of my Personal Space as a rim of Archangel Michael's bright blue light. Again, you choose whatever works best for you. It is your imagination and intention that counts.

You can add anything that you think may best support you to the boundary of your Personal Space. For example, you could add a mirror finish to your Personal Space so that whatever is not of Love and Light is automatically reflected back to its sender.

5. The Portal of your Personal Space

Within each Space, whether that be your Personal Space, your Work Space or your chosen World Space, there is what I call a Portal.
*(See **Diagram 2** p 12. Anatomy of a Personal, Work and World Space).*

The Portal is a very useful *one-way* space that I have created through which anything I wish to release from a Space can be posted and returned to the cleansing, healing, transforming Light of the Universe. You use a Portal to send anything you wish out of your Space and back into the Light.

The positioning of this Portal at any time is a personal choice, whatever feels best to you. It can be situated anywhere on the boundary of your Personal, Work or World bubbles.

I will often situate the Portal on the upper right boundary of a Space as this holds for me more a sense of the Light beyond. At other times I will choose to situate the Portal on a lower portion of my bubble boundary because this has more the feel of a dustbin for me, even though I know the other side of this Portal is also a return to the Light.

For example, when I finish connecting and working with others in a Work Space, I shall mentally send that Work Space off with thanks to The

Light to be enriched until next time, and also to clear my focus for the next Work Space I may choose to create and employ.

Another example would be if I were having a recurring unwanted thought or feeling about another or about an issue, I would send that other or the issue enclosed within its own Designated Personal Space out of my Personal or Work Space and into the Light through the Portal.

6. Add Creation Symbols

Choose what you now intend to consciously create or manifest and sketch these outcomes or end results as a symbolic form. These are your Creation Symbols and you place them at the periphery of your Personal Space. This serves as a quick daily visual and feeling reminder of where you are headed. Creation Symbols in your Personal Space also become like a postal address, a beacon to the Universe that spreads far and wide your intentions, where you can be found and where all your good can be delivered in a timely way. When you are looking for what may be the Next Best Actions to take to forward the fulfillment of your Creation Symbol's end result, it is best to do so within a Work Space. See p. 28.

7. Run The Light

It is a good opportunity at this point to do what I call, Run The Light through your Personal Space and the vertical cylinder of Light that you are now within – i.e. to see and feel this cleansing Divine Light moving downward and upward, washing through your physical, emotional and mental bodies, your chosen Creation Symbols and your Personal Space. *(See **Diagram 4** p. 17. The Vertical Flow of Divine Energy Through Consciously Created Spaces).*

This becomes like a meditation; an opportunity to spend some time to be in your own peace, to quietly experience being both in your human form (your body, mind and emotions) and also Divinely connected and protected.

The flow of Divine Light will continue to run through your Spaces even when you seal them. I choose that Love and Light, from whatever source, will always be given access through all my Space boundaries.

You can also Run The Light while lying down within your Personal Space if you choose. It is nice to feel the body supported by the ground and to feel the Light passing through it from the Earth Source.
*(See **Diagram 5**. Running The Light While Lying Down and While Upright).*

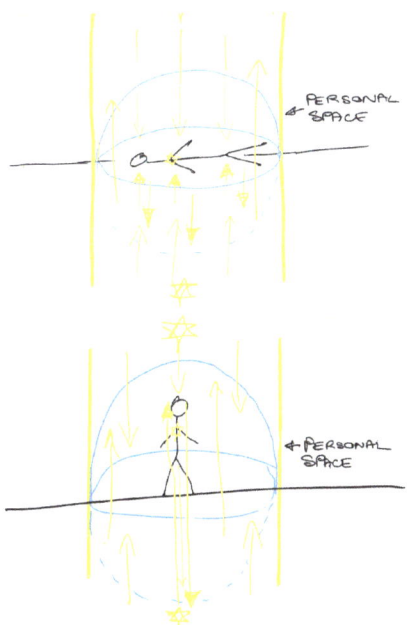

NOTE: The Light from the Earth Source can either <u>stop</u> at your head and return to the Earth for a more intense cleansing and healing effect OR the Earth Source Light can <u>pass on through</u> your physical body for an enriching exchange with the Heavenly Source.

<u>Diagram 5</u> Running The Light While Lying Down and While Upright.

Using The Breath

I find it a good idea to use my breath to accentuate the experience of Running The Light.

I take a deep breath in as I see and feel heavenly Divine Light run downwards through my physical body and Personal Space into the core or heart of the Earth below. Take another deep breath as I see and feel the Divine Light run upwards from the core of the Earth through my physical body and Personal Space back up to the heavenly Source.

After Running the Light upwards and downwards, it is also a great idea to breathe in Light directly from the surrounding space within the bubble that is your Personal Space.

After all it is also filled with Divine white Light. Furthermore, when you breathe in the Light from within your Personal Space you are then consciously acknowledging, owning and reinforcing the existence of your Personal Space for yourself. There are no rules; do whatever feels best for you.

Sometimes if I feel my physical body needs more support or grounding, I will run the Light from the core of the Earth up through my physical body from my feet to the top of my head and then back down again. You may notice that your feet begin to tingle as you consciously use your breath to cause greater connection with the Earth in this way.

Using a Mantra

Daily. Upon completing creation of my Personal Space, I shall daily (or as many times as I feel the need) recite my chosen mantras of:

'I choose Love, Light and Joy; Peace, Confidence and Trust.'

'I choose to be a compassionate, loving witness of my and others' human being.'

'I am powerful. I am a powerful co-creator.'

'Thanks Be To God.'

When my mind is very active or distracted. When I am finding it difficult to focus on the images and feelings of Running The Light, I will recite a specific mantra in my mind (or aloud if that works better). The mind can only do one thing at a time.

You can use any mantra that works best for you. My go-to mantra for this is:

'Thanks Be To God.'

As I breathe in from either the Heaven or Earth Source, I breathe in the mantra, as I speak it in my mind (or aloud). The mantra thus becomes the most prominent active part of the practice of Running The Light. Breathe in *'Thanks Be to God'*, breathe out *'Thanks Be to God'*.

8. Thanks be for the Creation of your Personal Space

WORK SPACE

Definition and Uses of a Work Space

A Work Space is a space you purposefully mentally create in order to connect through Source with others, or with your Creation Symbols. These connections can be with anything you choose. For example, it could be a connection with other people, or a project you may be working on, a desired outcome, a connection with an animal, or to the natural kingdom around you.

Rehearsal

This Work Space can be used as a rehearsal space, or a template of the visual and feeling perspective you choose to consciously bring to some future activity or interaction. As I did prior to visiting the dentist (p. 2).

Creation

Your Work Space is a great creation space too. It is while in this Space that you can bring focus to any project you are working on. All the Elements and Players for this project are brought together so that you can creatively move it along in the easiest, most confident and best way.

Peace

Your Work Space can also be used purely as a way to move through your day in a space that is kept clear in Love and Light while others may be moving through it. For example, while you are driving, or out shopping, while you are at work or at home, or while you are in a public space.

Acknowledgement vs Connection

There is a distinction between acknowledging another's presence and connecting with them. Acknowledging another is an awareness that they are passing through your Work (or World Space), whereas when you choose to connect with another you are consciously choosing to set up a Divine mutual link between you.

*(See **Diagram 6** p. 26. Acknowledgment vs Connection with Others)*

Security and Choice

If there is someone who makes you feel unsafe, or to whom you feel some resistance and you do not wish to connect with them in your Work Space at this time, you can also consciously and clearly choose to shut them out. A psychic hand – *'be gone'*.

Method

1. Use Archangel Michael (or other Higher Energy), or your imagination and intention to reset your Work Space boundary and to clear it with a blast of white Light.
2. In your mind's eye, see that other, *and* any unwanted energy they may be carrying securely enclosed within the boundary of *their* Personal Space.
3. Flood their Personal Space with white Light for their Highest Good. They may well need it. They can unconsciously then use this Light however they wish.
4. Send them a clear psychic message of *'no entry permitted or engagement wanted here; go in peace'* and in your mind, Post them through your Work Space Portal into the Light.

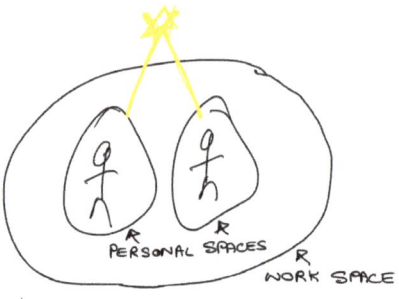

1. CONSCIOUS CONNECTION WITH ANOTHER IN YOUR WORK SPACE FROM WITHIN SEPARATE PERSONAL SPACES AND CONNECTED THROUGH SOURCE.

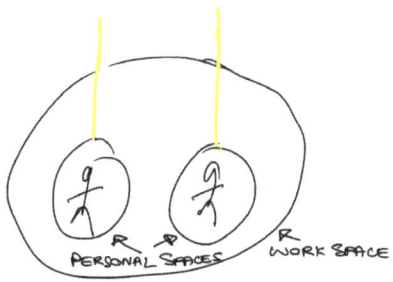

2. ACKNOWLEDGMENT OF ANOTHER PASSING BY IN YOUR WORK (OR WORLD) SPACE BUT CHOOSING TO HAVE NO CONSCIOUS CONNECTION WITH THEM.

Diagram 6 Acknowledgement vs Connection With Others.

Note: Maybe any resistance to that other is merely because they are activating something within yourself you are currently not ready to look at. You may well have a deal of Lower Energy Thoughtforms within your own Personal Space that you would rather be kept unacknowledged and stay unaddressed at this time. Thanks be to that other for alerting you to that and then send them on their way into the Portal with Love and Light.

Healing for Self and Others, Near and Distant

The Work Space can also be used as a healing space, for the Highest Good of all concerned. You would move the Healing Circle Designated Space into the Focus Circle at the centre of your Work Space.
*(See **Diagrams 2a–c**. pp. 12–13)*

When you are connecting with other people in this Work Space you can be connecting *in real time and space*, such as you would at a meeting or a consulting room.

You can also connect *in real time and separate space*, i.e. while both are in separate places, such as you would do for distant healing work.

There are many possibilities; such as using a Work Space to connect with loved ones who have passed over, or to investigate past lives, if that is your interest.

Respect

It must be said that respect for the Personal Space of others should be honoured at all times, both in terms of how that other may be choosing to use their Personal Space, and also in terms of gaining permission to connect with them in their Personal Space.

That is why all connections in your Work Space are only made through Source and by a mutual mental or verbal consent to the connection. As always, to be governed by whatever is for the Highest Good of all concerned and with thanks for the connection.

Remember, once you have finished working or playing within a specifically created Work Space to release all participants and this Work Space back into the Light through the Portal for the Highest Good of all concerned and with thanks.

If you are in doubt whether to work with another energetically, send them Divine white Light which they can then use or not, however they choose.

Method for Creating your Work Space

As with your Personal Space, the size of your Work Space depends upon how much space you feel you need, and will be comfortable within at any particular time. Use your imagination and intention or Archangel Michael (or another Higher Energy) to help secure the boundaries of this Space and to blast and clear it for you, and to set a perimeter that will be permeable only to Love and Light.

You would use the same steps as you did for making your Personal Space:

1. Claim

I would look to see how much physical space about me I feel I need or want at this time; claim and see, and draw a mental boundary of the room or area for your chosen Work Space in front of and around you, above and below.

Let this claimed space take a shape. It can take on any shape; it could be balloon-shaped or reflect the square or rectangle of a room. This is now the boundary of your chosen Work Space. If you would like to, you can ask Archangel Michael to help make and secure these boundaries for you.

2. Clear & Seal. Add The Portal

Use your imagination and intention or ask Archangel Michael to blast this Work Space with Light for any clearing and cleansing that may be required, and to seal this Space to entry from all but Love and Light. Create a *one-way* Portal somewhere on the boundary of your Work Space to receive all posted completed or unwanted energies back to the Light.

3. Connection

Because you will be working with others in this Work Space, see yourself (in your Personal Space) within this Work Space, then consciously create and introduce other Designated Spaces (p. 10) in the form of Personal Spaces, for other **people who are physically present** in this chosen Work Space. See all spaces linked through the connection each has to the heavenly Divine Source. These links will look like an energetic maypole.

*(See **Diagram 7**. The Energetic Maypole Within the Work Space)*

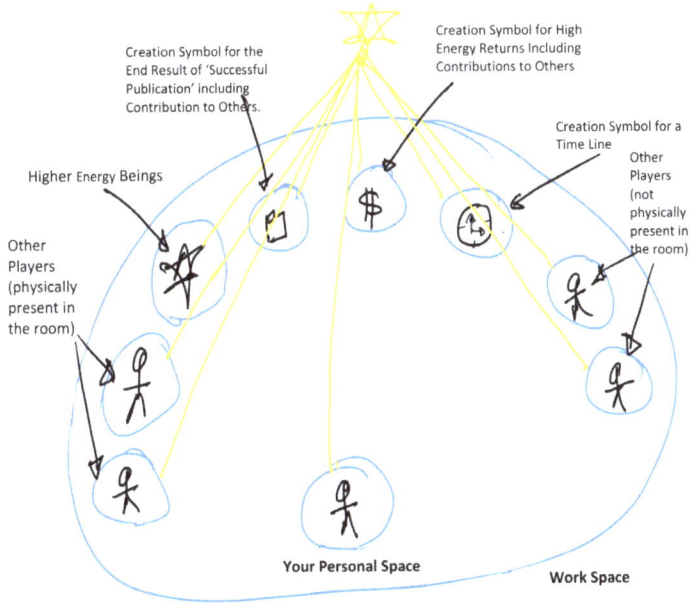

Diagram 7 The Energetic Maypole Within a Work Space Where Elements and Creation Symbols for your Chosen End Results are all Connected Through Source.

4. Introduce Creation Symbols and Other Supportive Players

A Creation Symbol is a simple symbol; a sketch I invent that represents all that I choose to create with regard to a project or an interaction. The symbol becomes like a quick, easy mental cue to all my intentions for creation in that project, or part of the project or interaction. It needs to be simple, easy to draw, and to mentally and emotionally call up. As such it is more schematic of nature, not a work of art. Connect each symbol to Source.

Other Supportive Elements or Players – those not physically present. I will want to include all other people or Higher Energies within this Work Space that I feel would most benefit me in the successful completion of the project or interaction that this Work Space has been specifically created for. Every Player will have their own Designated Personal Space within this Work Space, and be connected to Source.

Once set up, your Work Space will look like it contains a maypole of Light which is connecting and interconnecting Source to yourself, the Creation Symbols and to the other supportive Players.
*(See **Diagram 7** p. 29. The Energetic Maypole Within the Work Space)*

Note: I find it supportive to also include my Creation Symbols around the perimeter of my *Personal* Space so that they are a constant reminder of what end-results I am now choosing to co-create. In this way my Creation Symbols become like my personal beacon to the Universe – 'This is what I am now choosing to create for the Highest Good of all concerned'.
*(See **Diagram 8** p. 31. The Energetic Maypole Within the Personal Space)*

5. Run the Light

Run the light through the cylinder of Light that this Work Space now defines. In so doing you flush and make strong the heavenly and earthly connection of Source Light for all who are within your created sacred Work Space.

6. Thanks be

Thanks be for this Work Space and for all who have come together for the purpose of connection and creation.

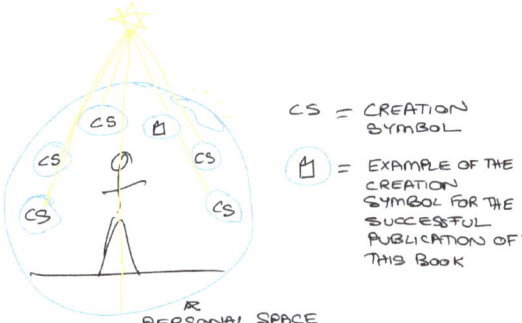

Diagram 8 The Energetic Maypole Within a Personal Space Where Elements and Creation Symbols for your Chosen End Results are all Connected Through Source.

7. Completion

When you have finished working within and have given thanks to your Work Space, send it off through the Portal into The Light to be refreshed until next time.

Method for Completion

1. Spend a few moments of connection and of thanks, take deep breaths of acknowledgment to all the introduced Elements; the Creation Symbol(s) and any Players.
2. Give the Work Space and all the Elements a blast of imaginary or of Archangel Michael's clearing, cleansing Light.
3. Run the Light through the team and the Work Space you are about to leave.
4. Declare *'It is done for now, until next time we gather and thank you'*.

5. Send this specially created Work Space off to the Light through the Portal.
6. Then on to another Work Space or not depending upon what you are working upon or engaging with. I will create specific Work Spaces for specific projects or interactions as required.

    I have a general 'go to' Work Space that serves to open any chosen area to only Love and Light, where others may pass acknowledged but with whom I will not consciously choose to connect with. See Acknowledgement *vs* Connection on page 25. For example, while out walking on a seaside footpath, I will open a Work Space where I can include and focus upon and breathe in the energy of the plants around me, the sky and/or the sea. Any passers-by are merely acknowledged but not connected with.
7. Thanks be.

....

Example 1 – Creating this Book in my Study Work Space

Before I began writing I would turn off my phone, then I would set up my Personal Space and then my Work Space which would include any Elements I felt would aid me in a confident, easy and successful writing process.

These Elements were two Creation Symbols and three Other Players.

Creation Symbols

Symbol 1: For the successful publication and life of this book as a contribution to others, including High Energy returns.

Symbol 2: For all those who would most benefit from this book. That they have a clear voice that lets me know what they most need to know and how to best express that – the right audience.

*(See **Diagram 9** p. 33. Creation Symbols for World Wide 1. Successful Publication and Contribution to Others of This Book and for 2. The Right Audience, readership)*

Diagram 9 Example: Creation Symbols for Worldwide
1 Successful Publication and Contribution to Others of this Book.
2 Right Audience, Readership.

Other Players

Player 1: Archangel Gabriel for the art of writing, knowledge and wisdom.

Player 2: A master of writing who has great clarity, wisdom and writes from the heart and with ease. The name of this writer I am not aware of at present, but it does not seem important for him or for me. I know that he is present and Thanks be. Interestingly as I proceed with writing this book, there seems to be a crowd of helper writers gathering in my Creation Symbol – a veritable party! Thanks be. Thanks be is my shorthand way of giving thanks and expressing my gratitude. It is not a reference to any religious dogma but may also include Thanks be to God.

Player 3: Collaborators. To include all those people who are or will be collaborating with me on the successful publication and distribution of this book.

Player 4: A Valkyrie helper to bring to my attention and to send off any of my Lower Energy sabotage Thoughtforms that may arise.

*(See **Diagram 10** p. 34. The Work Space for the Successful Writing of this Book)*

So, in my Work Space bubble while writing this book, there were five Elements, each in their own Designated Personal Space bubble. Me in my Personal Space and the four Elements mentioned above. We were all interconnected to the Divine through a maypole of Light. In this way

I trusted that all that I needed to say and how best to express it would be given to me. I see this book as a team effort linked through Source. Thanks be.

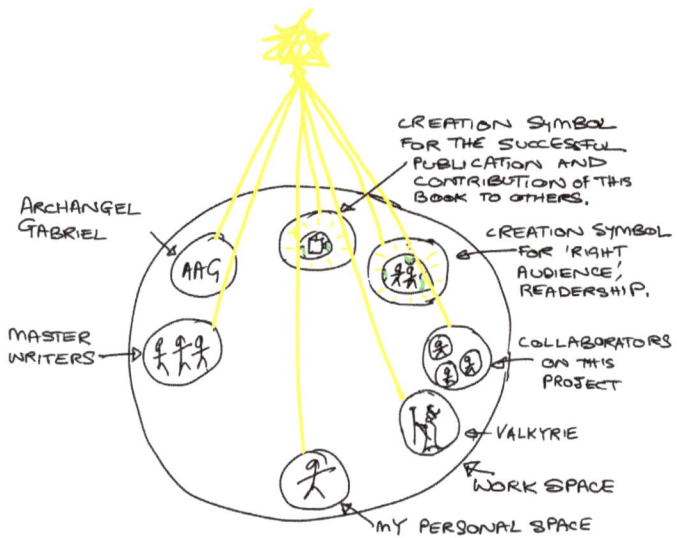

Diagram 10 Example: Work Space for the Successful Writing, Publication and Contribution of this Book.

The process once the Work Space for this book was created, was one of trusting my intuition, the still small voice of guidance within, and following that. In this way, writing and rewriting for greater clarity became an easy, timely and enjoyable process without any sense of pressure. Thanks be.

Example 2 – Meetings & Appointments

You could create a Work Space if you were going into a meeting with others, either face-to-face or via zoom etc; or if you had, say, a medical appointment. You can easily create a Work Space which is set up with specific intentions to forward optimal interactions and end results. You thereby create an environment that can proceed with most peace, confidence and trust, without knowing exactly how that may play out. Within this Work Space each player is connected to the Divine Source so that the best outcomes can become possible.

*(See **Diagram 7** p. 29. The Energetic Maypole Within the Work Space: Where Elements and Creation Symbols for your Chosen End Results are Connected Through Source)*

WORLD SPACE

Definition and Uses of a World Space

It is not always necessary to create a World Space, often a Personal and Work Space are sufficient. The size of any of your Spaces are always flexible. Sometimes I will expand my Work Space to the edges of my World Space. I will create a World Space for myself when I am driving, in a theatre, out walking in nature or in a shopping centre. Or I will create a World Space for a house. It is a Space we are choosing to include in our conscious awareness and to clear, seal, Run the Light, to connect and to feel at peace within.

It can be a Space in which, although there may be other people in it, we are *not* choosing to directly work with, or engage with them. It is rather a Space in which we can open our awareness, and where the mystery of Divine Spirit can whisper and bless us in unknowable ways. Thanks be.

Opening Up

It is a way of opening up our presence to a wider global view of the world about us. It feels like a psychic breath of fresh air to open oneself up in this way to a wider inclusive World Space. Often when I extend my World Space out, say to the horizon, I am often stunned by the magnitude of beauty that lives within it.

Ease and Relaxation

I find the advantage of looking to the horizon always gives me an immediate ease and relaxation in body, mind, and soul. A slow, full exhale and inhale. Thanks be.

Gift to Others

There is the added advantage that as we flood this wider arena of focus with Divine Light, we support not only ourselves but also all other beings who may be within it.

Size

A World Space can be any size one chooses, depending upon one's needs of the moment. It could be as far as the eye can see, the horizon or the confines of one's home, or maybe just a streetscape.

Nature

Within a World Space I find I become more aware of nature. This reminds me to acknowledge and commune with the plant, animal, and mineral kingdoms, to breathe deeply from these realms. This heals, informs, and nourishes all parties.

Mini-World Spaces

I will make mini-World Spaces for our home when we go away. I sometimes make them for the homes or modes of transport of our family and children. I create in my mind's eye a very quick boundary of Divine protective Light that encircles and clears them for the Highest Good of all concerned. I do this knowing I cannot change the course of life for another, but at least there has been a gift of Love and Light for all.

Planet Earth

We can create a World Space that surrounds and includes all or parts of our planet. We can consciously flood it with Love and Light for the Highest Good of all concerned without knowing what form that may take.

Method For Creating Your World Space

1. Claim

As you did when creating your Personal and Work Spaces; you decide and choose what size you wish or need your World Space to cover.

2. Clear and Seal. Add the Portal

Let a Divine boundary describe the extent of the World Space you now choose to be conscious and aware of at this time. Include a Portal for release of all unwanted, or no longer needed, energy and thoughtforms. Use your imagination and intention, or Archangel Michael (or other Higher Energy), to readily help you make this Space and to blast it clear of any lower energies that are not for the Highest Good.

3. Connect

See the conduit that this chosen World Space has opened up and that now directly connects all within it to the Divine Source above and below.

4. Run The Light

Let Divine Love and Light flow up and down this conduit to enliven, to heal, to enlighten all within it – human, animal, plant, mineral and spirit.

5. Thanks Be

Thanks be to Source and all who support the workings of Source. Thanks be to all the Elements within this World Space.

6. Completion

When you have finished working or playing within your chosen World Space and have thanked it for its support and given it a '*farewell, and until next time*' psychic wave, post it through the Portal at the boundary of this World Space and let it go back to and be transformed into The Light. No matter what size your World Space, there shall always be a bigger context or World Space in which it sits!

....
Example 1 – Driving

While driving, creating a World Space makes clear to me my intention of peace, relaxation, and safety for this journey.

My car becomes my Work Space; the traffic and streets about me, my World Space. This reminds me to stay conscious of the world around me and to who I am being as a driver; how I am feeling, to my reactions if any and to take responsibility for any lower energy that may arise.
....

....
Example 2 – Orchestral Performance

I am an amateur oboist and prior to any performance in an orchestra I would set my Spaces and intentions. I and all the other members of the orchestra were contained within our own Personal Spaces, interconnected through Source and then as a group held within an Orchestra Work Space. This would aid my focus, attention and acceptance of all musical outcomes for myself, for my fellow players, and for the music. The audience I would place in a separate Audience Work Space, each connected to Source. This provides the two-fold benefit of connected listening between the audience and ourselves as performers, and for the music to be received as a source of upliftment for us all. Both the Audience and Orchestra Work

Spaces lay within the perimeter of a World Space that I would designate to be the auditorium area. Sometimes I would extend my World Space for the performance to include the surrounding neighbourhood, so that the Higher Energy the orchestra and audience created together would be more widely available.

*(See **Diagram 11**. Setting Up Elements and Intentions for an Uplifting Orchestral Performance using Designated Spaces)*

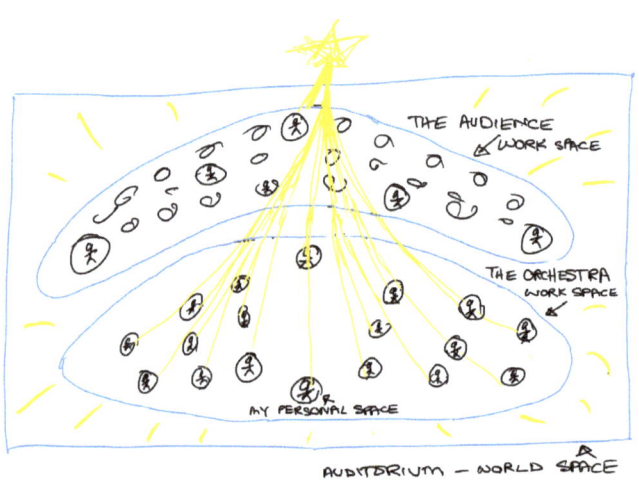

Diagram 11 Example: Setting Up Elements and Intentions for an Uplifting Orchestral Performance Using Designated Spaces.

SPACES AS A TOOL

By consciously creating Spaces and working with energy, you give yourself a tool for: Manifesting your chosen outcomes; A daily meditation practice; Right Relationship; Health Creation; and for Wealth Creation.

1. Manifestation Tool

It is possible to use consciously created Spaces to clarify, work upon and make manifest any desired end result or outcome you may choose.

It is always good when making goals to addend to your chosen end result:

'I now choose to consciously create…..(End Result or Outcome)……

or something better,

in the perfect way and at the right time,

for the Highest Good of all concerned.'

When you have consciously chosen your preferred end result or outcomes, you can turn these into Creation Symbols and add these to all your Spaces (Personal, Work and World). Any supportive Elements you would like to have around you should be placed within your Work or World Spaces only.

You can include a daily meditation practice around your chosen Creation Symbols and end results to enliven them and to inform you of any Next Best Actions to follow.

When you feel your end result or outcomes are stuck or delayed, or cause you reactionary thoughts and feelings, you can use an unravelling technique (p. 54, 58) to free up the manifestation process.

2. Daily Meditation Practice

Stillness You can have a daily meditation practice of Running The Light within your Spaces. A peaceful time of being silent and still within your Divine Spaces.

Energizing of, and Guidance from, Creation Symbols. You can have a daily meditation practice with your Creation Symbols and the chosen end results they hold, by sequentially bringing them forward into the Focus Circle at the centre of your Work Space, Running the Light through them and asking for any guidance or Next Best Actions they may have to offer you. This will energize and make these end results a brighter presence in all your Spaces, enliven your positive expectations and signal to the Universe where these formed end results can find you.

Chakra Clearing, Energizing & Sealing. As part of a meditation you can Run The Light through your chakra system. Run the Light from both the Heaven and the Earth Sources simultaneously to each chakra, one at a time. Begin with the base chakra and then move sequentially through the sacral, solar plexus, heart, throat, third eye, and crown chakras. To 1. Clear a chakra - run the collected white Light in an anticlockwise direction as many times as it feels necessary so that all that is of Lower Energy can be released and you can see only white light swirling out of that chakra; 2. Energize the chakra - let the collected Light from both Heaven and Earth Sources this time spin clockwise within that chakra. You will see the colour of that chakra flooding the area of the body around and out of it. I like to give the whole body a flood of this colour too. 3. Seal the chakra - place a closure motif over the chakra. I use a gold star form, you could use a christian cross, or something other, whatever has meaning for you. Keeping your chakras clear, energised and sealed can help support the well-being of body, mind and spirit.

3. For Right Relationship

I use the term **'right relationship'** to distinguish a relationship where each party is connected to the other through cords of Divine Source and that each party is doing so from within their own Personal Space. This style of relationship can exist even when only one player in the relationship consciously decides that both players shall inhabit separate Divine Personal Spaces. That is, whether or not the other person is aware of the creation of Personal Spaces, a Work Space or the connection of all through Source. How extraordinary would it be when both or all parties in a relationship consciously choose to relate to each other in this way?

There will be times, say in a public place, where you will be aware of others in your Work or World Space. You would still see all parties within their Personal Spaces as they pass through your Work or World Space, but you choose to not consciously connect with them through Source at this time.

*(See **Diagram 6** p. 26. Acknowledgment vs Connection with Others)*

I do not want to shut the world out in all its colours, but by using the tool of Spaces I can now more easily distinguish what is mine and what may be being directed at me from some other, or that I may be resonating with, and that now calls for me to own, experience and release. This 'other' may be another person or a passing energy or thoughtform.

Given that spiritually we are all One and that we all share the human condition, very often this will mean that what you feel, so can I. The degree of empathy I may have to you depends upon such things as my level of willingness to connect with your Personal Space, the degree of resistance I may have to your current emotional energy state or thoughtforms, and how conscious my inner sensitivity is.

Not good or bad, just worthy of note that when one finds oneself caught in a reaction, it is often wise to stop and reflect, to ask yourself some questions. Is this reaction energy mine? Is it me resonating to you? Have our Spaces collapsed into each other? Has some other low energy cloud passed nearby or attached to one of my Spaces?

*(See **Diagram 12**, p. 45. Personal Spaces in Right Relationship and When Personal Spaces are Collapsed, Either Consciously or Unconsciously. See **Diagram 3**, p. 15. Different Ways Lower Energy Thoughtforms and Reactions Can Be Given a Shape or Physical Form)*

The corollary to the oneness of all human beings is that whatever thought, emotion, action or Energyform I send another, I shall immediately and automatically be sending the same to myself. For there is no 'other'. We are all one. This is so whether the recipient other knows about it or not. The boomerang effect.

This can work in both directions. Disempowering, make-wrong or violent thoughtforms towards another or others will continue to resonate within **your** Spaces regardless of how right or deserved you hold them to be. So too shall any higher energy thoughtforms such as empowerment, love, compassion, kindness, forgiveness, acceptance and acknowledgement be similarly left resonating in your Spaces. Some call this The Law of Attraction. I call it a law of creation.

The value of being a conscious responsible human is that we can be either empowering and supporting others and ourselves or we can be heaping abuse and fear and make-wrong upon others and ourselves.

As an aside, I am always surprised that when say, as a car passenger I may idly be looking at another driver, most often that driver will turn and look back to me. How did they know I was looking at them? More evidence for me that we are spiritually linked human beings.

Ultimately the aim of a conscious human is to stay self-aware and to take responsibility within one's Spaces for oneself. Equally, we respect

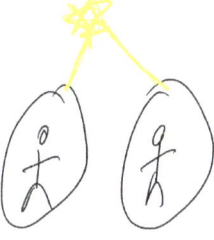
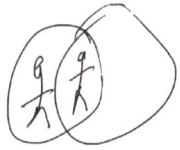

'Right Relationship' in Separate Personal Spaces 'Connecting' Through Source.

Unconsciously Collapsed Spaces, as in:
1. Co-dependency,
2. Dominating and Controlling or Intrusive Relationships,
3. Loss of Clear Self-identity and Choice.

Conscious Surrender and Collapsing of Personal Spaces for Mutually Agreed Intimate Relationship

Diagram 12 Personal Spaces in Right Relationship and When Personal Spaces are Collapsed, Either Consciously or Unconsciously.

and honour the power of others to be able to own and be responsible for their own Spaces.

I find the distinction, 'My business. Your business. God's business' a very useful one (*Byron Katie, "Loving What Is", p. 3*). We can have no idea of the experiences, or the lessons being presented to others, as painful as that may be for us to witness. We each have our own experiences and lessons to learn. We each are born with the same repertory of human thoughts and feelings, whether we allow ourselves to acknowledge and feel them or not.

Uses of Spaces and How to Objectify Energy, as a Relationship Tool

Gift of Love and Light

We can send Divine Love and Light to others to use however they choose; to aid their healing, peace, and resolution.

Self-Knowledge and Understanding

We can more accurately discern how energy forms are behaving around us and the effect they are having upon us.

Discernment

We can own what energy belongs to us and what may belong to another.

Personal Power

We can be responsible in our own Spaces and send unwanted energy on its way in the form of return sender or post it (p. 47) through a Portal to the Light.

Compassion and Forgiveness

We can have more compassion and be more forgiving of our fellow travellers and for ourselves.

It makes a big difference when we can be responsible for our own Spaces and choose to live intentionally and consciously in as much love, light and joy, peace, confidence, and trust as we can allow.

Perhaps we are a microcosm of the macrocosm of this world? If our microcosm shines more brightly with Light, then maybe Light shall also shine more brightly for all upon our planet?

Method for Using Space Creation and Energy as a Relationship Tool

1. Space Creation

Using Personal Spaces and a Work Space, it is possible to set your intention for the end result of any meeting with another or others. You can mentally preset the form of right relationship and mutual respect that this meeting shall take linking all with Divine cords of Light. You can see and feel the desired happy outcome for all concerned, and yet not know how this will be achieved.

In terms of personal connections, it is not respectful to try to force a quality or form of relationship with another to be in accord with your desires. You can set up a right relationship scenario, but this shall always include **free will**. You cannot know or decide for another the type of relationship or intimacy another wants or chooses to have with you, no matter how good your intentions. You can offer another loving conscious connection through The Divine but the quality and style of their connection to you is up to them. Right Relationship is about a mutual agreement. Respect.

2. Objectify Energy as a Form or Shape

So far, we have gathered the tools of Space Creation and the ability to objectify Energyforms or Thoughtforms as shapes (p. 14). This enables us to take responsibility for ourselves and to more easily unravel (p. 55, 58) and personally identify, understand, and work with the nature of the Energyforms that may be operating within our Spaces.

3. Enclose, Post and Return Sender

We can then proceed to enclose the expressed lower energy forms in a bubble of Light prior to sending them on their way to The Light through the Portal. This action of sending I call **'posting'** or **'post it'**.

When we feel we have been sent Lower Energy Thoughtforms from another, we can surround these Energyforms in a bubble of Light and '**return sender**' via the Portal. It is not for us to clear up others' Lower Energy Thoughtforms, to be their psychic or emotional dustbin. My feeling is that it is more appropriate that those others are allowed to own their own stuff, to be responsible for their Lower Energy Thoughtforms and to deal with them consciously whenever they are able. We may never know what life stresses are being experienced and suffered by another.

It is not about making another wrong for sending you Lower Energy Thoughtforms but rather to develop your skills to see it, to feel compassion for whatever may be going on for that other, to return sender of that Lower Energy Thoughtform back into *their* Personal Space, then to support them with a blast of Light into their Personal Space, and to intend that they with their Lower Energy Thoughtforms are posted into The Light for their Highest Good as soon as you part company. This can be repeated as often as necessary. *(See **Diagram 13**. Enclose, Post, Return Sender of Lower Energy Thoughtforms from 1. Another Person; 2. A Passing Low Energy Thoughtform Cloud)*

4. Next Best Action?

From within your cleared Personal Space, you can better see what your Next Best Action might be; words to speak, peaceful movement towards or away from another or to receive whatever valuable messages may come to mind to be shared, or not, as you choose.

5. Reclarify and reset any Personal or Work Space Boundaries, if necessary

For example, if you feel someone is intruding into your Personal Space, you would initially, in your mind, make it absolutely clear that you claim

Example 1: Having Angry Energy Directed at us by Another.

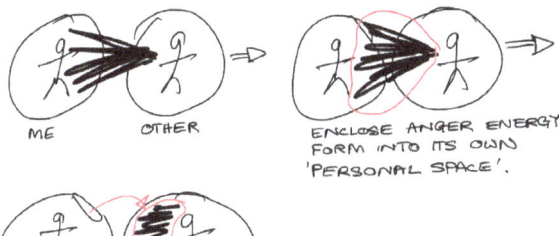

ME   OTHER

ENCLOSE ANGER ENERGY FORM INTO ITS OWN 'PERSONAL SPACE'.

USE PORTAL TO 'RETURN SENDER' ANGER ENERGY BACK INTO THE OTHER'S PERSONAL SPACE FOR THEM TO DEAL WITH.

Example 2: A Passing Low Energy Thoughtform Cloud 'Feeding' from Your Personal Space.

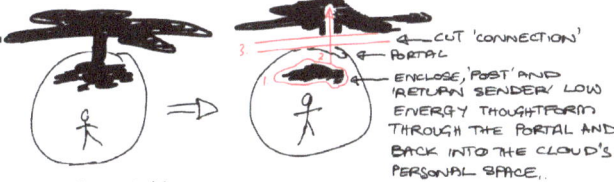

UNCONSCIOUSLY 'CONNECTING' WITH AND 'FEEDING' A PASSING LOW ENERGY THOUGHTFORM CLOUD.

CUT 'CONNECTION'
PORTAL
ENCLOSE, 'POST' AND 'RETURN SENDER' LOW ENERGY THOUGHTFORM THROUGH THE PORTAL AND BACK INTO THE CLOUD'S PERSONAL SPACE.

LOW ENERGY CLOUD MOVES ON AND AWAY.

Diagram 13 Enclose, Post, Return Sender of Lower Energy Thoughtforms from:
1 Another Person.
2 A Passing Lower Energy Thoughtform Cloud.

and allow only right relationship, i.e. you see yourself and the other are connected only through The Divine and in your *separate* Personal Spaces and that further, any conscious connection between you shall occur only when you choose. In your mind you have psychically spoken to this intruder; '*back off, be gone*'.

*(See **Diagram 6** p. 26. Acknowledgment vs Connection With Others)*

You can also post any person out of your Work or World Space through a Portal and into The Light if you so desire.

*(See **Diagram 12** p. 45. Enclose, Post, Return Sender of Lower Energy Thoughtforms)*

From the position within your Personal Space and within your chosen Work Space, you are then best empowered if you choose, to use your voice to clearly speak yourself, your authority, and your needs.

Remember, the best action may be to remove yourself physically from the person or situation whenever it is possible to do so.

6. Thanks be

Example 1 – A Work Meeting Presentation

You have decided to give a talk at work, but you are feeling waves of insecurity about it, not good enough, inadequate for the task, shy, fearful of being publicly humiliated, getting it wrong, failing, rejection, losing your job etc., etc. There could be a range of Lower Energy Thoughtforms and emotions connected to, prior, during and after this talk.

1. *Objectify the Energy – in your Personal Space*. What form would these thoughts and feelings take if you gave them a shape? Draw it out, write out any other thoughts and feelings that may come up with this drawing.
2. *Objectify the Energy – in your Work Space*. You may have a whole range of reactions and beliefs, real or imagined, that you feel and hold about

the others who may be at this planned meeting. Give these lower energies a shape. How are they affecting, acting upon you? It could be like a wall of not listening or make-wrong or it could take the form of spears of ridicule. As you draw it out your emotions will clarify the shape and content of these Lower Energy Thoughtforms.

3. *See and feel the Desired End Result within your Work Space.* On a separate drawing, sketch how the ideal outcome would look and feel; the smiling faces, nods, congratulations, interested questions, thanks, a sense of delight, accomplishment and relief for yourself, or a mantra *'that was fun and easy'*; to any others whose Lower Energyforms may be active within their Personal Spaces, you can send them Light so that their lower energy stays contained within their Personal Space and can have no effect on you. 'I see and feel you, but this is your stuff, be in peace'.

4. *Enclose and Post it.* Return to the initial sketches. Use your pencil to enclose the Lower Energy Thoughtform shapes in their own Divine bubbles of Light. Draw an arrow from each bubble, which then becomes like an action pointing it into and through the Portal, and on into the Light to be transformed back into the Light.

5. *Reset your Personal and Work Space, including any Next Best Actions* as you now choose it to be. Draw it if you would like to reassert this for yourself. You could add any other Elements (be that Creation Symbols or Players within their own Personal Spaces) into your Work Space that you feel may support you in this upcoming meeting. During the meeting, there may be some recurring wobbles back into Lower Energy Thoughtforms; see it, post it, reassert the truth of your chosen end result, and if you have one, repeat your chosen mantra for the event. Trust in the meeting's own miraculous perfect unknowable path and outcome.

6. *Thanks be.*

Example 2 – Driving cont.

While driving, I can readily experience reactions of impatience or judgement. It can be so easy to let one's attention wander causing one's responses to the present to be clouded with a mental and emotional swirl of unresolved thoughtforms about past or future situations, people, possibilities, hopes and fears.

Often one can be present to receiving and reacting to Lower Energy Thoughtforms, and reactions from other drivers. For example, when I think I can feel the anger and impatience of the driver behind me. It is a relief not to have to pick up and carry these Thoughtforms. There is always a choice.

The easy way to return to balance, peace, and safety on car journeys is to stay **aware** of what Thoughtforms and Energyforms may be coming up for us and then to ask the questions about the possible origin of these feelings. A reminder to oneself that the purpose and **intention** of driving is to get somewhere peacefully and safely, not to swim in all the possible emotional conditions available. If they do not belong to us, make the choice to **enclose and post** any or all of these Lower Energyforms to the Light for transformation through a Portal. **Return Sender and Peace be with you**.

For example, when I notice I have slimed (mentally sent another a Lower Energy Thoughtform) another driver with angry and make-wrong thoughts, I'll apologize in my mind. Then I'll see the Lower Energyform, that I have just plastered on the person and their car, enclosed in a Light bubble. I post it to the Light and give the other driver a farewell blast of Light to take into their day.

If I am the receiver of a plastering and know that I have been slimed with a Low Energy Thoughtform by another driver; I shall immediately return sender the Energyform; then see the driver and their low energy securely contained within their Personal Space. I then put their car into a clear and separate Work Space; shut down any conscious connection between us; send them on their way and in my mind post them out of my World Space. We do not have to connect with other people, it is our choice and gift.

*(See **Diagram 6** p. 26. Acknowledgment vs Connection with Others)*

....

4. For Health Creation

Best Medical Practice

Before I begin, please be reminded that whatever tools I present here, must always be used in conjunction with only the best medical practice and not as an alternative to professional medical support.

Self-responsibility

We are all a part of this dance we call a human life. We always work best as a co-operative team while simultaneously being under the empowering umbrella of personal responsibility. We each come with our own unique skills to share and to support each other.

I am going to use a current passing health issue to show you the ways in which you can use Space Creation and Energy work to help support relief. You can use techniques such as unravelling; seeking, listening to, and acting upon your inner advice; seeking and listening to the whispers of Spirit that bring further understanding of the energetic causes or links to your body issues; breathing in the healing energy of the plant kingdom and from the World Space.

These are all methods of objectifying the dis-ease one is experiencing in the body. You can take responsibility for a health situation in a wholistic way, that is to look at how it is affecting your body, mind, and emotions by giving the dis-ease a shape. Instead of surrendering to being a victim to your health dis-ease, you are giving yourself more power to manage and work with understanding whatever can be done to best support your body and energy systems at this time. What are the lessons contained within the current health challenge? As always, it is one step at a time and with trust in the Divine process, and being self-responsible. **Note:** Seek professional advice when appropriate.

Growth

By engaging in this kind of enquiry you open yourself up to, and develop your confidence and trust in your personal inner listening skills, and in your connection to your body's wisdom, and to the wisdom and guidance of Spirit. As well as using the Space and Energy tools here, other activities such as walking, being in nature, meditation, or the words of another can aide you to stay open to your own best wisdom.

....

Example – Neck Jam

I have been experiencing a somewhat painful and tiring neck jam at the base of my neck. When I stop and lie or sit down it usually goes away. I have tried a number of healing modalities to no avail, including medications. I feel reluctant at present to venture into a doctor's surgery, go to an osteopath or a physio. I will definitely do so if needs be.

I am curious to know why my body feels it needed to adopt this affliction. I also feel that this dis-ease is an opportunity for me to take responsibility for it and to interact with it directly. In this way I can allow it to reduce or leave. It is about my taking responsibility for, and empowering myself to make a difference, instead of immediately giving that power away to others. That is, I need to first understand what is the gift of learning this neck jam holds for me? Thanks be. The following techniques were used over a number of days.

....

Method For Unravelling, Using a <u>Healing Meditation</u>

Unravelling is a term I use to represent the process of clarifying what may be going on energetically within one's Spaces that could be causing a felt reaction within one's mind, emotions, or body.

A **healing meditation** is a particular form of meditation in which I use a hands-on approach to my, or another's, etheric double within a purpose-created Healing Space. This Healing Space is a Designated Space that I bring forward from the periphery of my Work Space, and place into the Focus Circle at the centre of my Work Space. This Work Space calls together especially selected Players who are Higher Energy healers and if the healing is for another, will include any other Higher Energies that may wish to and/or are already working with that other. *(See **Diagrams 2a-c**, pp. 12–13)*

I use my physical hands to direct and deliver the Divine Light that travels through me and to see and understand what may be energetically going on for that other, be that for myself when I am the client, or for another. I am using my hands like eyes, to see what may be going on for another.

A healing meditation was the first thing I gave to myself as a form of enquiry and healing.

In this healing meditation, I witnessed that I could barely see myself within my Personal Space. It seemed cloudy and obscured. I was puzzled to see this, as it was not something I had seen before. As I looked more closely I could see what looked like silk curtains that extended from ceiling to the ground, behind which I was hiding. I could also see that behind these curtains I still shone brightly. I just didn't want anyone else to see me shine so brightly. Maybe it was a past life memory of being at risk if I was seen as bright and powerful.

It doesn't really matter if this is true or not. Rather it is a visual scenario that can be worked with and that makes sense at some level.

I could feel what looked like daggers in my back and neck area. With the help of my other Higher Energy workers within my Work Space, I used my hands to etherically take them out and reassured this Diana that she was safe, and that it was safe to let herself and her talents shine. We then encouraged her to drop her silken veils and to post them to the Light. It was time for her to come out of hiding, to stand proud, confident and at peace in her Light and power. I used my hands to help energetically post these veils back into the Light.

We then gave her the mantra to recite whenever needed: *'It is safe to be seen, to speak my truth, to shine my Light, to shine brightly'*.

I also used my hands to give an energetic treatment to parts of Diana's etheric body for healing and for the balancing of energy. This is similar to what one would do in an intuitive reiki-type session.

Letting oneself shine seemed to be the theme of this healing meditation for myself. The words 'to not hide oneself under a bushel' came to mind. To stop hiding my light; hiding myself and my talents from view. How apt. To share myself in this way; my beliefs, thoughts, and the ideas within this book have indeed been a giant leap for me. Hiding has meant that the writing and publication of this book has been greatly delayed for many years.

Breathing in Nature from Within My Work and World Spaces

As I walked along the seaside the following day, I could still feel an ache in my neck, so I decided to ask the plant kingdom to cleanse and heal whatever was out of balance in my body. I didn't know what needed to be done but I trusted the power of the plant kingdom to bring the right healing for me. I consciously included the plant kingdom around me into my Work Space as I walked. I breathed deeply of the plants from root level up to the sky and then back again through my physical body from within its Personal Space.

Similarly, I took deep breaths from within my World Space that extended to the horizon. This open breath to the horizon is always such a source of relief.

On this day I was becoming uncomfortably hot while on my walk. I had dressed for winter with a skivvy and a shirt. It has been my way for many years now to dress in layers, hiding what I felt were my unacceptable bits. In the past I would have just tolerated this overheating until I returned home to change into lighter clothing, i.e., to a lighter undershirt!

After the previous session of unravelling my neck-jam, it occurred to me that all of who I am is good enough. There needs be nothing for me to hide. I can shine brightly and beautifully whatever the shape of my body or the clothes upon it!

I reminded myself that this body, my Personal Space, Work and World Spaces are created solely for me and for my enjoyment. These are my Sacred Spaces of Love, Light and Joy, Peace, Confidence and Trust. I choose to bring approval and allowance into them for myself and for others. How many years have I lived these words as my truth, yet only now does it open up to be more fully appreciated and enjoyed. Thanks be. I am always learning. Thanks be to you body.

Yes, I took off my outer shirt ... and scarf. I walked proud and sprightly in the warm sunshine beside the sea. I honoured my body and well-being. I let go of any sense of shame, and caring what others may think of my body. Thanks be.

At some point walking along the sand, my neck became more painful again. The words *'take a seat, have a rest'* came to mind and so I did. I stretched my spine as I sat to gain relief. I felt a click. It came to mind that this is the part of my spine that I may have been holding tight, to 'looking good, looking and being good enough' and that it was now released, or in the process of releasing. Now that it was freed and more mobile, it needed more muscle support around it. It then came to mind to use a lightweight stretch band to develop and strengthen muscles in this area of my back.

So, **the lessons** of that day's walk was that I had been hiding with clothes my sense of not being good enough. That fear of being found out as not being good enough had created fear and a protective rigidity in my upper back and that there is something I can do about it. I can stay aware when I fall into this old habit of hiding myself away in whatever way that may be. I can exercise in certain ways; I can listen to and be more responsive to my body; I know that within my Personal Space there shines a brilliance that is Diana who resides in this physical form and has her particular talents. I may not know exactly what these talents are, but I let them express themselves in whatever way they do – brightly. Thanks be.

My upper back issues at this point seem to be all about being good enough or fearing that I am not good enough.

Method For Unravelling Using a <u>Drawing Technique</u>

The next day my neck pain persisted somewhat, so I used a series of questions combined with a sketching technique to further unravel what I needed to know and learn, in order to release what feels like stuck energy from my upper back.

These are copies of the sketches I made at that time in order to show you the unravelling process. **Note:** No artistic talent is required to successfully use the Drawing Technique as a tool.

*(See **Diagram 14** p. 61. Example – Neck-Jam. The Unravelling Process Using a Drawing Technique)*

1. What is So Now?

With regard to my neck and back, 'How does it feel?', 'What are the Lower Energy Thoughtforms doing to, or about me?'

I roughly sketched out how it felt. It felt like I'm stopped in my tracks and bent over with the effort of trying to move forward; there are daggers in my upper back and a hook in my back which is firmly secured on a taut line holding me in place. In front of me is an impenetrable wall with a clear STOP sign upon it. I do not know what all this is trying to stop me from, other than from moving forward. I wonder is this a warning or an obstacle?

2. What Do You Choose to Create Now?

I sketch my ideal outcome, what I would like or prefer to be so now and note any thoughts that come to mind e.g., free and easy movement, open path towards all my Highest Good and towards all my consciously created end results.

*(See **Diagram 14** p. 61)*

3. What Do I Need to Do Now?

I sketch these out.

*(See **Diagram 14** p. 61)*

1. **Post it.** Post anything unwanted, such as the wall and the STOP sign.
2. **Messages or A New Mantra?** What do I look like now? I see a picture of myself standing tall with a new mantra that has come to mind and to follow:

   'I am free to move forward on my path towards my Highest Good with confidence, peace and freedom'.

4. Next Best Action?

1. **Breathe** and scan the physical body,
    Run the Light through this new condition.

    I breathe from this new position and scan my body for how it now feels. I notice quite a degree of relief, but there is still some discomfort below my right shoulder blade. I give it a shape and post it.

It comes to mind that this issue arises from fears I hold with regard to the safety and wisdom of sharing my life and these techniques with others.

2. **Add Creation Symbol.**
*(See **Diagram 14**)*

I add the Creation Symbol for this book into the sketch of the chosen end result of walking my Divine path

3. **Further Messages or Mantras.**

These further messages or mantras then come to me:

'It is safe to share my truths, my life and my methods with others for the Highest Good of all concerned'

'Only those who can benefit from, and are open to this sharing, will receive this information and book'

'I trust that Source makes my way and the way of this book safe and clear. Thanks Be to God'.

'I walk upon a Divine path of Love and Light towards the End Result of this book being successfully published. Thanks be.'

5. Breathe and Run The Light

As I sit here, I use my imagination to position myself upon this idealized Divine Path with the End Result of this book shining bright. I Run the Light through this Creation Symbol and breathe deeply in the freedom, confidence and trust I have while on this Divine path.

6. Thanks be

With this unravelling technique, I can now clearly see and understand the great stress to my body of this inner conflict of pushing forward with writing this book while at the same time unknowingly having my psychic brakes full on!

1. What Is So Now?

'Daggers and hook and taut line in my upper back'

2. What Do I Now Choose to Create?

'Free and easy movement towards my chosen end results and Highest Good'.

3. What Do I Need to Do Now?

a).

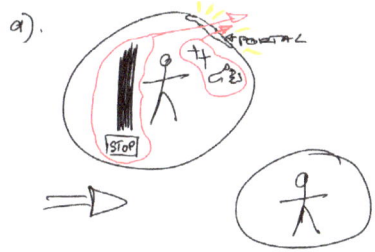

MESSAGE:
'Stop, stand tall and consciously remove these impediments'.

'My way with peace, confidence and freedom'.

b). NEW MANTRA:
'I am free to move forward on my path to my Highest Good with confidence, peace and freedom'.

ACTION:
1. I make a new Creation Symbol for the successful publication of this book.
2. I 'see' myself moving freely towards this chosen end result.

c). Adding a Book Creation Symbol brings up my fears about sharing my truth. The following mantras (see text) then come to me: 'It is safe...', 'Only those who can benefit...', 'I trust that...', 'I walk upon the Divine Path...'.

Diagram 14 Example – Neck-Jam. The Unravelling Process Using a Drawing Technique.

It also occurs to me that the gift of my body's aches and pains is indeed to stop me, to keep me in place at the writing desk, focused and completing this book, no distractions!

My neck and back ache resolved into a peaceful condition. If this neck-jam does return, I shall take it as my body's sign to slow down, to not rush, to stop pushing so hard towards whatever it is I may be engaged in. Thanks be.

5. For Wealth Creation

Wealth Creation brings together all the aspects we have covered so far; Space Creation (p. 10), Running The Light (p. 20), Creation Symbols (p. 10, 28), Objectifying and Working with Energy forms (p. 14), unravelling (p. 55, 58), posting (p. 47), asking questions, listening for answers, mantras, following guidance.

Wealth Creation covers all the end results or outcomes that you have consciously chosen to make real; it is abundance in whatever form you choose. It could be an abundance of health, a career choice, a type or quality of relationship, a particular home or a sought-after income or windfall. Abundance means different things to different people, and at different times in their lives. There is no limit to the type and quality of abundance you can choose to create and to real-ize for yourself.

If your attention is on creating abundance for others, or for this planet, it is proper in terms of respecting free will, to offer up the bounty of non-specific Divine Light to shine fully upon whomever you would like to support energetically. They are then free to use the gifts of Divine Light and Energy however they choose.

The object of this book is to leave readers empowered in their own lives as conscious powerful co-creators with The Divine and in being self-responsible for the quality of their energy.

Method for Creating Wealth

Space Creation – Your Personal Space

Make your Personal Space and Run the Light through it. Breathe 10 or so breaths in both directions or whatever feels sufficient for you. See and feel the Light energy pass through your physical body.

Space Creation – A Work Space

Method

1. **Make Your WorkSpace.** Create your Work Space and see yourself connected to the Divine from within your Personal Space within this Work Space.
2. **Add Elements.** Introduce whatever Player elements (contained within their own Designated Personal Spaces) you feel are going to support you best in this Work Space and put them around its perimeter. These Players could be people (alive, passed or mythical) or Higher Energy beings such as spirit guides.
3. **Creation Symbols.** Choose or create the Creation Symbols that relate to the desired function of this Work Space, and that you wish to energize and receive guidance from. Place these Creation Symbol(s) also around the perimeter of this Work Space.
4. **Connect** each Element, Player and Creation Symbol to the Source. You are now connected energetically through Source with each of these Elements and Symbols and are ready to ask questions and listen for the answers from each of them.
5. **Run The Light** through this Work Space. Include yourself and the Elements and Creation Symbols within it. Breathe 10 or so breaths from above and below to clear and energize all within this Work Space. See and feel the Light energy as it passes through this Space.

Working With Your Creation Symbols

As you stand looking into your Work Space, bring forth into the Focus Circle of this Work Space (this is in a central position and in front of you) a Creation Symbol of choice. In this way you are choosing to connect and work with a particular Creation Symbol and all the conscious choices you have made for the end result or outcomes that it holds within it. It can be helpful to keep a list of all your Creation Symbols with a dated, brief written description beside each in a small book, such as a repurposed address book. This will be a ready reference tool for you.

Method

1. **See, Feel, Speak**

   See and feel all the outcomes that this Creation Symbol represents. Speak your conscious choice to yourself aloud or silently;

   'I now choose to create .... or something better, in perfect ways and at the right time for the Highest Good of all concerned. Thanks Be.'

   By seeing, speaking, and feeling your end results in this way, you reacquaint yourself with this chosen end result in its real-ized form.

2. **Next Best Action?**

   Now, ask this Symbol what is the Next Best Action I can take in order to bring the end result it represents into my life? It may be for no action or you may receive a clearer feeling or picture of your chosen end result when real-ized, or there may be a particular action suggested; a person to call or something other.

   Note: sometimes the actions suggested will seem unrelated to the outcome you are seeking. Trust and go with it.

   There will be a message for you of some kind. Even if there seems no clear guidance, the mere act of revisiting and spending time with your intended end result activates, revitalizes and energizes it. Your clear, committed intentions makes it easier for your chosen end result to find and to move closer to you, to be made manifest into your world.

We are powerful co-creators with the Light. The more Love and Light we can bring to whatever creation processes we use, the quicker your chosen end result can be realized.

*(See **Diagram 16** p. 71. The Effect of Being on Different Energetic Highways for Manifesting Outcomes and End Results)*

3 **Releasing Lower Energy Thoughtforms from Creation Symbols**

It can be easy to **fall** into low energy thoughts and feelings about our intended or desired end result. After all, they are not present in our lives – yet!

The nay-sayers within and without, abound around the topic of fulfilling one's dreams and notions of the power of possibility. For many it is easier to cry *'get real', 'that's not how the real-world works', 'there's no such thing as this magical thinking', 'be reasonable, it's all and only about hard work'* etc., etc… For some it is easier to not explore or try on the possibility of something greater operating in their lives; to avoid the disappointment of failing to create.

These Lower Energy Thoughtforms are indeed a fall, for they cloud the visibility of our Creation Symbols and all that they represent from the Higher Energy that will have them be real-ized and made manifest.

Method for Releasing Lower Energy Thoughtforms from Creation Symbols

1. Objectify (p. 14) these Lower Energy Thoughtforms – give them a shape and see, feel, and hear how they are affecting your Creation Symbol.

2. Unravel (p. 58) the low energy effects using the drawing technique, or in your imagination, while connecting with the Creation Symbol in your Work Space.
3. Post any unwanted Lower Energy Thoughtforms.
4. Messages, Next Best Actions or Mantras.
5. Re-Speak what you are consciously now choosing to create. Speak and write down any new mantra truths that are pertinent to this Creation Symbol.
6. Run the Light over renewed Creation Symbols and
7. Thanks Be.

....

Example – Unravelling For the Successful Sale of Our Home Using a Drawing Technique.

*(See **Diagram 15**. Sale of Our House. The Unravelling Process Using Drawing Technique)*

....

1. What Is So Now?

The Creation Symbol for selling our current home contains an image of its new owners coming to our door with an acceptable purchase offer. While working with this Creation Symbol I saw a cloud of not good enough hanging over our current home. That cloud held all the overwhelm I see and feel with our home's faults and repair needs; all the places in the house and in the garden where I feel it is not good enough, cared for enough, or needs repairs and is generally not up to standard.

I let my reaction express itself by drawing a giant black cross right over this Creation Symbol accompanied by a flood of my low energy verbiage that went with it:

Spaces As A Tool

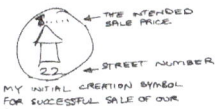

MY INITIAL CREATION SYMBOL FOR SUCCESSFUL SALE OF OUR HOUSE

1. **What is So Now?**

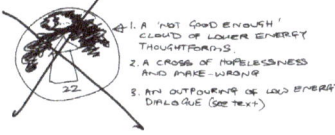

2. **What Do I Now Choose to Create?**

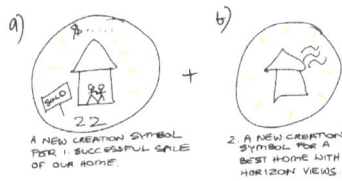

3. **What Do I Need to Do?**

a) 'Post' dark cloud from my Creation Symbol.

b) MESSAGE: *'See only love and...'(see text).*

c) 'Post' the dark reactionary cross-form.

d) MANTRA: received, *'All things are...(see text).*

e) ACTIONS: 1,2 & 3 (see text). Run The Light.

Diagram 15 <u>Example</u> – Sale of Our House. The Unravelling Process Using A Drawing Technique.

> *'That's just not possible, shame on you, get real Diana, join the real world, it's just not going to happen, you're wasting your time if you really want to sell! Silly magical thinking, unrealistic to the max!'*

For many, these are logical albeit stern words of reality and wisdom. If you want to sell your home you normally go to a real estate agent, etc. This does seem like me pushing possibility to the max, but I am very committed to the possibility of possibility and our power to co-create *whatever* we choose!

When you have drawn and written all that comes up for you about 'what is so now', leave it to one side and move on to:

2. What Do I Now Choose to Create?

What would you rather? I redrew and clarified a successful sale to a couple who arrive at the front door of our shining current home, which included raising glasses of champagne. How civilized! It is always valuable to add more joyous feeling into the images of our end result. In so doing we energize the power of our Creation Symbols.

3. What do I need to do now?

Post 1. I posted the dark cloud from around the Creation Symbol into the Portal and I got the message and mantra to:

> *'See only love and appreciation for your current home, including all its less than perfect bits.'*

I see the wisdom in this, for in letting go of making my current home bad and wrong, I lighten the energy around it and make it immediately available and more attractive to its new owners; let alone more enjoyable for the time I am granted within its walls. The prospect of doing work on it now seems more approachable and enjoyable. I can be within it with thanks and appreciation for all of what is.

Post 2. I posted the Lower Energy forms of the black cross and the words away from my Creation Symbol and into the Light of a Portal (p. 67).

A new mantra to speak when with my Home-Selling Creation Symbol:

'All Things Are Possible in God, The Light'

'Thanks Be'

4. Next Best Action?

1. Dustbin. I feel the need with this particularly strong negative low energy outpouring, to tear up the drawing of what is around this Creation Symbol and throw it in a physical dustbin or even better burn it in a fireplace. Done. I really don't need this low energy around the sale of our lovely home!
2. Champagne. I diarize to purchase a bottle of champagne and let it take pride of place in my study in anticipation of the successful signing of sale documents here in this lovely home. Done.
3. Re-Speak the end result held within my Creation Symbol. Now that the Creation Symbol has been cleared, I am able to powerfully re-speak, to reassert and claim for myself what I now choose to create and any new mantras relating to this Creation Symbol:

'I now choose to create the easy and smooth sale of our home in its current form for $..... (for an amount I have decided) in a perfect way and at the right time, and for the Highest Good of all concerned.'

'Our home is beautiful and stunning and I see and feel only love and appreciation for it, including all its less than perfect bits.'

'All Things Are Possible in God, The Light.'

'Thanks Be.'

5. Run The Light over this renewed Creation Symbol.

6. Thanks Be

A note on choosing end results

1. Set your Chosen End Result but not the how.

    In this case, it was also impressed upon me the possibility that even though these buyers are received at our door, this does not explain how this scenario comes to be.

    For example, they could indeed be at our door as a result of a walk-in enquiry off the street (my preferred scenario), or they could be being introduced to us by an agent, or they could merely be completing the sale in our home with some as yet unknown pre-story. I am happy with any how, it is the end result of a sale that is important for me.

    There is power, freedom and ease for yourself in releasing the how to the Universe. We are co-creating with The Divine, we can put our trust and confidence in The Light to know the best ways to deliver and manifest all our chosen end results and outcomes. Our job is to choose what we want to co-create and then to keep the energy as high and light as possible in the interim until it is made manifest in our lives.

    It is my belief that it is only upon the Higher Energy highway that all our chosen, desired and unexpected, delightful outcomes and end results will travel to us and be made manifest in our lives.
    *(See **Diagram 16**. The Effect of Being on Different Energetic Highways for Manifesting Outcomes and End Results)*

2. …this or something better and that is for our Highest Good

    There may be many delightful, unexpected surprises that the Universe may have in store for us and wants to deliver to us.

Allowing for '…this or something better and for our Highest Good' makes it possible for us to receive all our intended good, whether we consciously called for it or not.

Thanks be.

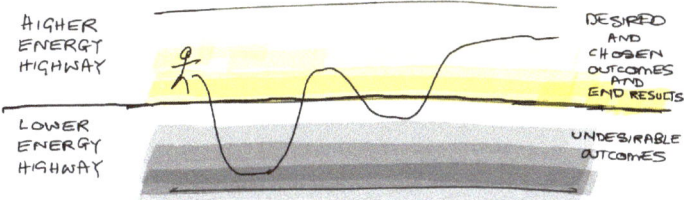

Diagram 16 The Effect of Being on Different Energetic Highways for Manifesting Outcomes and End Results.

DIVINE TIMING AND CONCLUSION

I choose to believe that there is a Divine plan at work in our lives, with opportunities and perfect timing operating for each of us and for each of our chosen end results.

Maybe the timing of the Divine Plan depends upon how readily we allow ourselves to experience and to learn the lessons that each accomplishment, manifestation, or life stage offers?

Maybe what we judge as the right time is but a name we give to the outpouring of our controlling, fearful ego selves demanding results from our limited human vantage point? We cannot know what truly is in our best interest. Either what is for the best in terms of a chosen end result or the best timeline for our chosen outcomes. What we think we may want; we may later realize is not what we want or would choose.

We are able to acknowledge, trust and have confidence in Source and to surrender to a greater Truth; that there is a Divine Mystery at play right now in our lives that is constantly orchestrating for the Highest Good of all concerned.

In the light of this, there is much value when making goals to remember to addend:

'I now choose to create...... (end result)...... or something better, in the perfect way and at the right time for the Highest Good of all concerned.'

Maybe The Divine Plan is purely for us to consciously real-ize our true spiritual selves, and to experience the Truth of the flood of Love and Light that is for all time? For me, that is a continuum – there is always another level of Light to know and allow, and *many* times I fall.

My human is often predominant, and I become lost. Eventually the pain and discomfort of living outside my Truth will cause me to recognise the fall and remind me to do the work using the tools of Spaces and Energy; to externalize and objectify my reactions as forms on a page, to thereby gain greater clarity and relief, to take energetic and if necessary, real time inspired action. Always with compassion and forgiveness for the human condition that I live within.

In conclusion, all that I share is my truth only and is a way that helps me to make sense of this world and how best to navigate it with personal responsibility and power. It empowers me to hold to the beliefs that it is possible to consciously choose my path, that **all** there is Is Love and Light and that Divine Source connects and supports each of us and this planet.

I am by nature a very private person, but I choose to share with you my truth and some of my personal journey in the hope that perhaps some of it may be useful for you as well.

I wish you great success and an amazing adventure if you do choose to try on these Space and Energy techniques. If you do, I would love to hear how successful you find them. Please take full responsibility for your own well-being all the while.

I am sure you and I will further refine what works best for us in our lives.

Be brave, share **your** truths and talents, for you make a difference and your wisdom and skills advance us all.

Seek The Light for yourself, others, and this planet.

With Love Always, Go Very Well,

ABOUT THE AUTHOR

Hello my name is Diana Renee McLellan, and I have had the gift of this body for 71 years. I was born, educated and continue to live in Melbourne, Australia. I greatly enjoy being a sister, wife, mother and grandmother. Indeed this book began its life as my gift of possibility and love to my children.

I have studied at tertiary level law, psychology and business studies but life events led to degrees in none. I have an abiding interest and am a keen enquirer into things esoteric, the metaphysical, personal development, nature, creativity, possibility, art and music.

I believe that Love and Light is all that there IS and that each of us is a Divine Spirit housed within the form of a physical body.

My intention is to be a contribution to others, to stay cognisant of the Divine in all about me, to keep learning and discovering, expanding the possible and to enjoy all this life in Love and Light. Always with thanks.

For more information
or to order copies of this book please visit

www.lighways.com.au

or email the author

info@lightways.com.au

For your notes

For your notes

For your notes

www.ingramcontent.com/pod-product-compliance
Lightning Source LLC
Chambersburg PA
CBHW051540010526
44107CB00064B/2790